A MEDIEVAL MONK

Giovanni Caselli

PETER BEDRICK BOOKS

New York

Contents

Introduction

This story is set in the great monastery of Cluny in eastern France, in around AD 1140. The monks who lived there followed the Rule of St Benedict, a strict timetable which guided every part of their daily lives. St Benedict had been the Abbot, or head, of a monastery in southern Italy. He lived about 500 years before this story takes place. He did not like the way the monks in his monastery behaved, and so he drew up a set of guidelines, called his Rule, to help them lead better lives. Some of the monks found the new Rule too strict, and tried to poison him. But later, many people came to believe that St Benedict had been right. His Rule had helped the monks to live in peace with one another in their monastery, and to devote their energies to the service of God. Other monasteries were soon founded, and their monks followed St Benedict's Rule.

The monastery at Cluny was founded in AD 910. The monks were given land belonging to Duke William of Aquitaine. The land had been his favorite hunting ground, but he was persuaded to give it to the monastery by the first Abbot, whose name was Berno.

The monks at Cluny did not follow St Benedict's Rule exactly. St Benedict had said that monks should spend part of their day in church, praying and singing psalms, but that they should also work hard to support themselves by growing food and tending animals. But by 1140, when this story begins, the monks at Cluny no longer thought that work was important. Instead, they believed that most of their time should be spent worshipping God. So they employed servants and other helpers known as lay-brothers, to do the hard work for them.

This book tells the story of a young boy's first months in a great monastery. At the end of the book you can see some detailed pictures of the beautiful objects monks made and used in their daily lives.

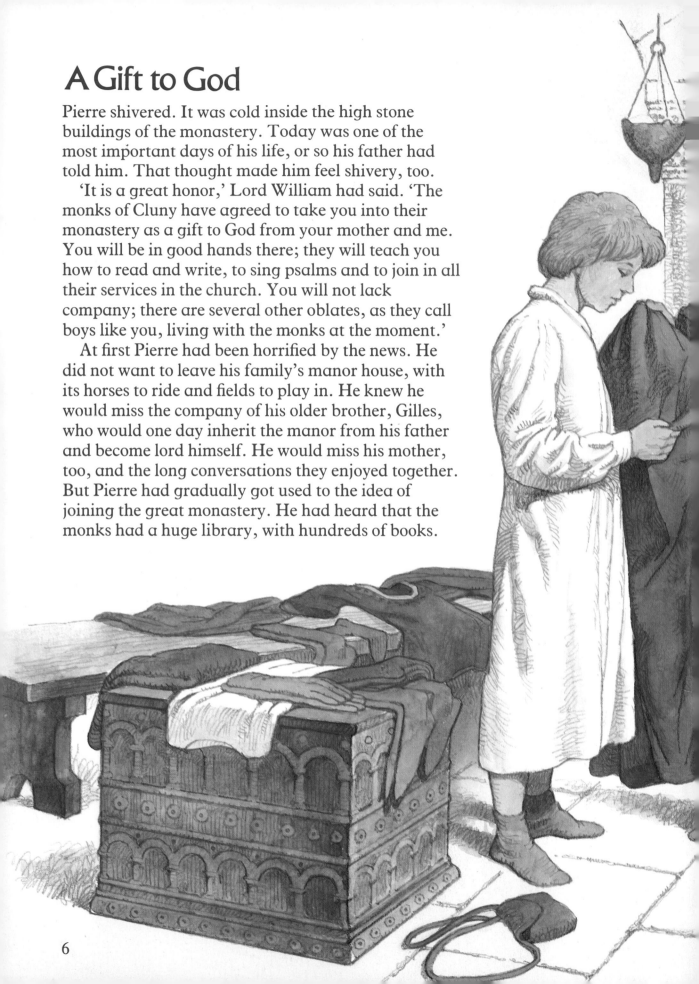

A Gift to God

Pierre shivered. It was cold inside the high stone buildings of the monastery. Today was one of the most important days of his life, or so his father had told him. That thought made him feel shivery, too.

'It is a great honor,' Lord William had said. 'The monks of Cluny have agreed to take you into their monastery as a gift to God from your mother and me. You will be in good hands there; they will teach you how to read and write, to sing psalms and to join in all their services in the church. You will not lack company; there are several other oblates, as they call boys like you, living with the monks at the moment.'

At first Pierre had been horrified by the news. He did not want to leave his family's manor house, with its horses to ride and fields to play in. He knew he would miss the company of his older brother, Gilles, who would one day inherit the manor from his father and become lord himself. He would miss his mother, too, and the long conversations they enjoyed together. But Pierre had gradually got used to the idea of joining the great monastery. He had heard that the monks had a huge library, with hundreds of books.

He looked forward to being able to read them, and perhaps to meeting some of the famous scholars who travelled to the monastery from distant lands. And, who knows? One day he might be a scholar too.

Now his home seemed far away. He stood nervously in his shirt as Brother Bernard, the monk in charge of the young boys, helped him into a small-size monk's robe, or habit, made of scratchy black wool. His parents looked on proudly, while a monk wrote down details of their gift. As well as Pierre himself, they had given two hectares of land and a silver bowl to the monastery. Pierre looked across at them, and at the stern figure of the Abbot, who was head of the whole monastery. He felt he was leaving one life for another life. He tried to smile, but couldn't help feeling nervous. Now he was inside the monastery walls, what would the new life be like?

Life in the Monastery

It had been a busy day. Pierre sat down heavily on his bed in the boys' dormitory and breathed a deep sigh of tiredness. Once his parents had left, Brother Bernard had introduced him to another boy, who looked about twelve, a few years older than Pierre himself.

'This is Denis, who comes from a village not far from your home,' Brother Bernard said kindly. 'He will show you round the monastery, and tell you something about our way of life. You're both excused from keeping our vow of silence for today, but don't go making too much noise!'

Denis had done as Brother Bernard suggested. They had been all over the monastery. Pierre was surprised to find it such a big and busy place. As well as the church and the monks' living quarters, there were workshops, barns, kitchens, storerooms and, of course, the library. Pierre was also surprised to see so many people who didn't look like monks.

'Those are lay-brothers and servants,' Denis had explained. 'We spend most of our time in prayer and employ other people to help us with the heavy work. The lay-brothers take vows of a sort, but they are not so strict as the monks' vows.'

At various times during the day, bells had rung to call them to attend services in the church.

'I'll never remember where I'm meant to be at any one time,' said Pierre. 'It's so confusing!'

'Don't worry,' replied Denis. 'You'll soon get used to our routine. Now it's time for bed, but there's a night-time service, so we have to get up in the middle of the night and get dressed again for church.'

'Don't the monks get sleepy?' asked Pierre.

'Sometimes they do. But one of the brothers goes round with a lantern to make sure no one is asleep. Now, goodnight, and be careful,' added Denis, as Pierre pulled up his habit a few inches to scratch an insect bite on his ankle. 'Don't let anyone catch you doing that. Monks and boys aren't allowed to show their bare legs. The Rule says that we must be neat and decent at all times.'

9

Pilgrims

Pierre had begun to settle in to the daily routine.

'Let me see, now,' he said to Denis, 'have I got the order of services right at last? We get up at dawn to sing Matins and Lauds. Then, an hour later, there is Prime, followed by a special service to pray for the dead – our brother monks and other people. Two hours later, we go to Tierce, and three hours after that comes Sext. Then there's another gap of three hours before it's time for Nones.'

'Well done!' said Denis. 'What comes next?'
Pierre shook his head. 'I can't remember.'

'Listen, then,' said Denis. 'After sunset we sing
Vespers, and then, after dark, Compline, which
means that the day is over. But you forgot the very
first service of the day, Nocturns. That's the one we
get out of bed for in the middle of the night. Now
hush, here comes Brother Martin. He'll be cross if he
catches us talking.'

'What are you two whispering about over there?'
called Brother Martin, sternly. 'You should be in the
schoolroom with Brother Paul. Idle chatter is an
invention of the Devil. Don't let me catch you
gossiping again!'

Pierre started to protest. 'It's not fair,' he said,
'Denis was only helping me to remember the names of
the services.'

'Don't bother!' hissed Denis. 'He's a miserable old
creature, always finding fault. Come along, I'll race
you to the schoolroom!'

They ran across the courtyard, ignoring Brother
Martin's shouts of indignation. As they approached
the main gate, Pierre stopped in surprise. He heard
loud laughter and cheerful voices. They came from a
group of brightly-dressed travellers who were talking
to the gatekeeper.

'They're pilgrims, I expect,' said Denis. 'We get a
lot of them. Some make the trip to the monastery to
show that they are sorry for their past sins. But a lot of
them, like this bunch, just use the journey as an
excuse for a holiday. Occasionally we get some rather
shady-looking characters, on the run from something
or somebody. Just look at that man over there, for
example. I bet he's got something to hide!'

In the Dining Room

'By the saints, I'm hungry!' exclaimed Pierre.

'Sshh!' came a warning chorus from the other boys seated at the table. Denis whispered to him, 'Watch how we make signs to one another, instead of talking. You'll soon learn them and then you'll find that you can make yourself understood even without words. See, if I wanted to ask Jacques over there to pass the fish, I'd wiggle my hand like this.' He made a sign like a fish swimming through water. 'But, worse luck, it's not a fish day today.'

Pierre missed the rich food that he had enjoyed at home. When Denis first told him that the monks were only allowed one meal a day in winter he was appalled. How would he manage?

'Don't worry,' Denis said. 'We boys also get a snack of bread and wine mid-morning. And when summer comes, and the days are longer, then everyone gets two meals, at midday and in the evening. It's not too bad.'

'Don't we ever have meat?' asked Pierre, longingly.

'No. Only monks who are ill are allowed to eat meat. But we always have three different dishes at dinner times. First we have dried beans, boiled and salted. Then there's cheese or eggs, cooked in several different ways. I like fried eggs best! And the third course is always vegetables, fresh from the garden.'

'And there's always plenty of bread,' added Jacques, 'and wine, too. And don't forget, Denis, that we have fish twice a week on Thursdays and Saturdays as well as on feast days.'

'Silence!' called Brother Bernard. He always ate with the boys, to make sure that they behaved. The other monks had a separate dining room. There were two kitchens, as well. In one, the monastery servants cooked the fish, eggs and cheese. The monks used the other one for preparing and cooking vegetables. Every monk had to take his turn as helper there, from the Abbot to the oblates.

'It's hard work, but there's always the chance of a bit extra to eat!' said Denis.

Maundy Thursday

A few days later, Pierre and Denis, with the other boys, were taken out into the monastery courtyard to watch the special Maundy ceremony. They followed the Abbot over to the Hostel, where beds and food were provided by the monks for any poor people who called at the monastery.

Brother Bernard explained the ceremony to the boys. 'We hold a ceremony rather like this every Sunday, when we monks wash the feet of the poor people staying in the Hostel. We do this to follow the example set by Jesus, as it is recorded in the Bible. But today's ceremony is different. Instead of giving money to the poor, each monk hands over his old shoes to the man whose feet he has washed. The poor are always grateful; they would have to go barefoot otherwise. To replace his old shoes, each monk is given a new pair by the Chamberlain. They are meant to last him a whole year, until next Maundy Thursday.'

Denis whispered to Pierre, 'I don't think anyone would want my shoes, do you?' The two boys giggled but then tried to look serious as Brother Bernard went on.

'As you know, we are given new clothes – habits, shirts, underpants and socks – at intervals during the year. Our tailors make them in the monastery workshops. We also get sheepskin cloaks with hoods, and fur-lined boots and gloves. We need them, too. It can get bitterly cold in the church in winter.'

Pierre tugged at Denis's sleeve. 'Look, isn't that the suspicious-looking character you pointed out the other day? He was with a group of pilgrims then. I wonder what he's doing here again?'

'You're right!' Denis agreed. 'He doesn't look like the other poor people to me. That's an expensive cloak he's wearing, and the bag he's carrying is made of good leather. Let's keep an eye on him if we can!'

Just then, Brother Bernard turned and frowned. They were obviously not paying proper attention to the Maundy ceremony. Both boys hurriedly stood still, with their heads respectfully bowed.

'Bother! We'll lose sight of him now!' whispered Denis. 'What a nuisance!'

Inside the Chapter House

The steady drone of a man's voice filled the room. From where they were standing, high up in the gallery, Pierre and Denis could see one of the monks reading from a large book. The other monks sat quietly, listening.

This was the first time that Pierre had been inside the Chapter House.

'It's called the Chapter House,' Brother Bernard had explained, 'because the monks read a chapter from the Rule of St Benedict before they start their discussions. The monks meet there every day, and ask each other's pardon for anything they may have done wrong. They can also accuse each other of bad behaviour if they have good cause.'

The reading from the Rule of St Benedict came to an end, and the Abbot stood up to speak.

'I have a very serious matter to report,' he said. 'There has been a theft in the monastery. Not long ago, we were given a fine silver bowl by the parents of one of our new boys. The bowl has disappeared, along with some other valuables.'

There was a murmur of dismay from the monks.

Suddenly Brother Martin leaped to his feet.

'Father Abbot,' he said, in an excited voice, 'I also have something to report. It's a case of continued bad behaviour. Who knows, it may even have something to do with the disappearance of the silver bowl! It's that boy Denis. He's always chattering and laughing, and is very disrespectful. I wouldn't put it past him to have taken the bowl, just as a silly prank. I was saying to some pilgrims who called at the monastery only the other day that he was a bad influence on the other boys, and that they ought to keep their eyes on their belongings when he was around.'

The Abbot frowned. 'Aren't you being a little hasty, Brother Martin?' he said. 'Young Denis is certainly high-spirited, but that doesn't mean that he's a criminal. We need proper evidence before we go accusing anybody. And it's very wrong of you to have spoken like that to people from outside the monastery. You know what the Rule says.'

Books and Manuscripts

Denis was very miserable.

'Don't worry,' Pierre said. 'No one else thinks you've taken the bowl. You heard what the Abbot said.'

'I know,' said Denis, trying to smile, 'but until that bowl is found, suspicions are bound to remain. But never mind that now. Come with me. I want to take you to meet Brother Gregorius.'

'Who's he?' asked Pierre, following his friend.

Brother Gregorius was in charge of the monks who copied and illustrated beautiful books and manuscripts.

'Does everyone work on copying manuscripts?' asked Pierre. He thought it would be wonderful to be able to produce something as lovely as the books that were lying around the workshop.

'Not all of us,' replied Brother Gregorius. 'But we are all taught to write in the same way, so that several brothers can work on one book. A few of the brothers are specially good at writing. The Abbot sometimes lets them stay here to finish their work rather than attend services, because he thinks it is important to produce beautiful books to glorify God and spread the Church's teachings.'

Pierre reached out and fingered the pages of a book that lay on a nearby desk.

'Don't touch!' whispered Denis, hurriedly. 'That's parchment, and it's terribly expensive. It's made from the skins of young animals – lambs and kids mostly. Look, you can see Brother Gervase mixing some paint over there. He makes it from the roots and leaves of plants. Sometimes the illuminators use gold leaf, but that's only for special books.'

'What are illuminators?' asked Pierre.

'They are the monks who paint the little pictures, called illuminations, next to the words on the page, or else decorate the page with beautiful patterns. Only a few brothers are skilled enough to do that.'

19

20

First Vows

It was a very solemn occasion. A group of novices were making their first vows.

'As well as oblates, like you,' Brother Bernard had said to Pierre, 'we also have novices living at the monastery. Becoming a novice is the first step towards becoming a monk. If a novice keeps his first vows, and obeys the Rule of St Benedict, then after several years, if the Abbot agrees, he can take his final vows and become a monk. Oblates are given to the monastery by their parents, but novices come to the monastery of their own free will.'

Pierre looked at the men taking their vows and wondered whether he might one day be in their place.

'Now,' Brother Bernard continued, 'the novices who are making their first vows today are quite a mixed group. There are some oblates, but we also have a couple of young men who have decided to leave the sinful pleasures of the world outside and to devote their lives to God within this monastery. There are also some older men, who wish to end their days in prayer. We even have a knight, who is tired of fighting, and who wants to live in peace and tranquillity from now on.

'First of all, the novices will be led into the Chapter House. The Abbot will meet them there and ask them whether they are quite certain that they want to join our Order. If they all say yes, then the Abbot will explain to them just how hard a monastic life can be. He will tell them that they will have to obey the Rule, however difficult it might seem. The Abbot will remind them that they will not be allowed to own anything except their clothes and one or two personal items. Indeed, from the moment they make their vows, their lives will no longer be their own. Everything they do must be to the glory of God, and not for their own benefit.

'There will then be a special service at the church, and finally, they will receive a special haircut, called the tonsure, when a bald patch is cut at the crown of their heads. This shows everyone that they are now no longer the same as other men; they are on the way to becoming monks.'

Out in the Open

It was early summer. The days were growing warmer and Pierre thought longingly of the outside world. He was beginning to enjoy living in the monastery, but sometimes he missed his former way of life. On a fine sunny day like today, he thought, he and his brother would have ridden out on their favorite horses for a good day's sport in the open air. He also missed watching the crops growing in the fields, and the orchards and gardens of his family home. He was delighted, therefore, when Brother Bernard told all the boys to meet him by the gateway leading to the monastery's orchards after their midday meal. They were going out to help the gardeners with their work.

Pierre looked around the gardens eagerly. The fruit trees seemed to be growing well, and the vines, too. But now that he looked more closely, he could see that one or two of the vines were leaning right over, and were almost flat on the ground.

'Let's go and have a closer look at those,' he whispered to Denis. 'I wonder what's wrong?'

22

They walked across the orchard to a small row of vines on the edge of the great vineyard.

'Look,' said Pierre, 'something's been digging at their roots! That's why they're leaning over.'

'Some small animal, trying to make a burrow, I expect,' said Denis, looking bored.

'Perhaps,' replied Pierre, bending down to examine the plants. Suddenly he scrabbled frantically at the soil with his bare hands.

'Whatever are you doing?' asked Denis, surprised.

'Hey, look at this! Help me dig!' gasped Pierre. 'There's something buried here!' Sure enough, the silvery gleam of metal showed through the dark earth. It was the missing bowl! With it were some other precious objects – a golden cross, a jewelled book cover and a little bottle made of solid crystal.

'Brother Bernard! Come here quickly!' shouted Pierre, completely ignoring the rule of silence. 'We've found the missing treasure! This proves that Denis isn't the thief, doesn't it? He'd hardly help dig up his own stolen goods! But I wonder who did bury them here?'

23

In Disgrace

On Sundays, people from the town came to worship at the monastery church with the monks. This Sunday, as they walked across the great courtyard, they saw one of the brothers standing by the church door, bare-headed and bare-footed. One of the monastery servants was standing beside him.

The barefoot monk was Brother Martin. This was his punishment for having spread false rumors about Denis to people from outside the monastery.

Pierre saw him as he came out of church with the other boys. He had been angry when Brother Martin called Denis a thief. But now he couldn't help feeling rather sorry for him. Some of the townspeople were snickering as they passed him.

'Why is the servant standing there too?' Pierre asked Denis.

'He's there to tell anyone who asks exactly what Brother Martin has done wrong,' replied his friend. 'It will make him feel very ashamed. That's part of the punishment, of course, and a very painful part. I'm sure he'll be careful about what he says in future.'

'He won't be punished any more than this, will he?' asked Pierre. 'Surely he has suffered enough?'

'Well, he might already have been called to stand up and apologize in the Chapter House, and he might even have been beaten in front of the other monks. His punishment would have been worse if he had committed a more serious sin, such as showing anger, quarrelling, or speaking to a woman. Then, he'd be sent to stay in a cell on his own. He'd have to stand at the church door during services, with his hood over his face, and he'd have to lie face down on the ground as the monks passed by until they had all left the church. This would show that he was an outcast from the community.

'Probably, no one would be allowed to speak to him either, except the monk sent by the Abbot to lecture him on his wicked ways. He would only be allowed to join the rest of the monks again when the Abbot was convinced that he was truly sorry for what he had done.'

Final Vows

'Just think,' said Denis, 'we were right all the time! The thief *was* that evil-looking man we'd noticed hanging about the place. Some of the monastery servants saw him in the vineyard. They chased and caught him, and he soon confessed to the crime. He must have come into the monastery with the pilgrims, then hidden himself until he could sneak into the church when it was dark. He probably made his escape with the crowds of poor people who came to the services on Maundy Thursday. He had hidden the stolen goods in the vineyard and had come to collect them. If it wasn't for your passion for fresh air and gardening, we might never have found them!'

'I still think it's a bit hard on Brother Martin to be punished so severely, though,' said Pierre.

'Ah, but the Rule of St Benedict *is* strict,' replied Denis, suddenly looking serious. 'It's there to guide us away from the many temptations to evil. The Rule only punishes people who disobey it in order to encourage the rest of us to lead better lives.' He laughed. 'Heavens! I'm beginning to sound like a monk already! Come on, we must go and get ready for the great ceremony in the church.'

Everyone in the monastery had gathered in the church to see the senior novices make their final vows. They entered the church in a slow procesion. Each carried a scroll of parchment with his vows written on it. Brother Michael, the master of the novices, read each set of vows in a loud voice, for everyone to hear. The novices promised to lead a life of poverty, chastity – they would have nothing to do with women – and obedience to the Rule.

The Abbot blessed the novices, and led the prayers. He preached a short sermon, reminding everyone present of the importance of the vows the novices had just made.

'Let us pray,' he said, 'that they may live good and useful lives in our great monastery according to the rule of the wise St Benedict, to the greater glory of God.'

Picture Glossary

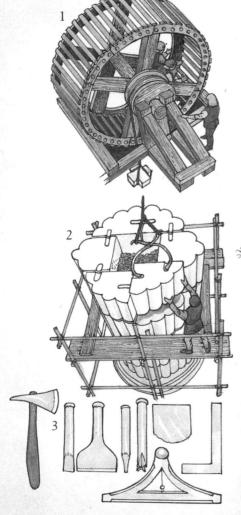

Above: A novice takes his vows and receives his monk's habit. The devil now leaves him.

The monasteries of medieval Europe were sometimes very large. They provided a living for many people. Many monasteries owned great estates, which they ran efficiently. They used the profits from their estates to build beautiful churches and other buildings. Cluny, the monastery in this story, was rebuilt and enlarged several times. The drawing (**below**) shows Cluny as it would have looked round about AD 1150.

The building was carried out by skilled masons (below left). They used wooden pulleys (1) to hoist stones to roof level. Pillars were built by bolting stone sections together with iron bars and filling the central core with rubble (2). The tools used by medieval masons (3) have hardly changed. No one has been able to invent a better way of working with stone since that time!

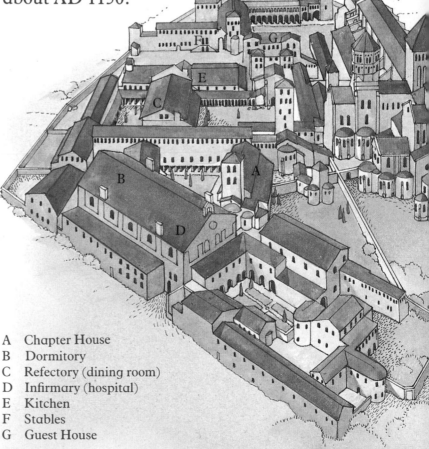

A Chapter House
B Dormitory
C Refectory (dining room)
D Infirmary (hospital)
E Kitchen
F Stables
G Guest House

28